FREE THE GALAXY

Written by Himani Khatreja

Penguin
Random
House

Editor Himani Khatreja
Art Editor Nathan Martin
Editorial Assistant Rosie Peet
Assistant Art Editor Akansha Jain
Jacket Designer David McDonald
DTP Designers Umesh Singh Rawat, Rajdeep Singh
Pre-Production Producer Marc Staples
Pre-Production Manager Sunil Sharma
Producer Louise Daly
Managing Editors Simon Hugo, Chitra Subramanyam
Managing Art Editors Neha Ahuja, Guy Harvey
Art Director Lisa Lanzarini
Publisher Julie Ferris
Publishing Director Simon Beecroft

Reading Consultant Linda B. Gambrell, Ph.D.

Dorling Kindersley would like to thank
Randi Sørensen, Paul Hansford, and Robert Stefan Ekblom
at the LEGO Group.

For Lucasfilm
Executive Editor Jonathan W. Rinzler
Art Director Troy Alders
Story Group Rayne Roberts, Pablo Hidalgo, Leland Chee

First American Edition, 2015
Published in the United States by DK Publishing
345 Hudson Street, New York, New York 10014

Page design copyright © 2017 Dorling Kindersley Limited
A Penguin Random House Company
17 18 19   10 9 8 7 6 5 4 3 2
006–283212–September/2015

A catalog record for this book is available from the Library of Congress.

ISBN: 978-1-4654-3794-5 (Hardback)
ISBN: 978-1-4654-3793-8 (Paperback)

DK books are available at special discounts when purchased in bulk for sales promotions,
premiums, fund-raising, or educational use. For details, contact: DK Publishing
SpecialMarkets, 345 Hudson Street, New York, New York 10014
SpecialSales@dk.com

Printed and bound in China

A WORLD OF IDEAS:
SEE ALL THERE IS TO KNOW

www.dk.com
www.LEGO.com

Contents

The Evil Empire

An evil Empire has taken
over the galaxy.
It is using its mighty army
and powerful starships
to bully helpless citizens.

Anyone who dares to speak up is punished. Is there anyone out there brave enough to stand up to the Empire and free the galaxy?

Dark Lords

Just hearing the names of
Emperor Palpatine and
his apprentice, Darth Vader,
can make people tremble.
These Dark Lords have
taken charge of the galaxy.
They love rules and making
life hard for anyone who
breaks them.

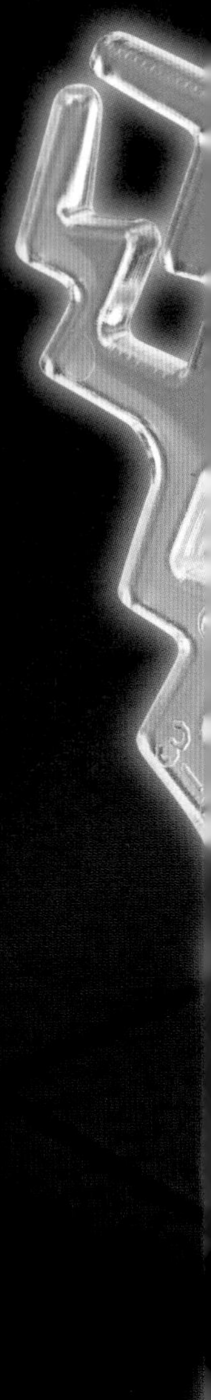

EMPIRE

Volume IX

BREAKING NEWS

The Empire Turns 14. Celebrate or else!

The Emperor looks radiant in his trademark black.

TODAY

By *Empire Today* Reporter

It was 14 years ago today that the supremely intelligent and handsome Emperor Palpatine took over the galaxy. He has ordered all citizens to celebrate Empire Day and say nice things about the Empire—or else. Speaking on the occasion, the Emperor said, "Each of you insignificant mortals is lucky to have a ruler like me. Now go away!"

"I will destroy anyone who dares to rebel against the great Emperor."

—*Darth Vader*

"The Emperor is our leader. Errm, he is always right. Usually..."

—*Brave stormtrooper*

The Jedi

Once, the Jedi warriors were
protectors of peace and justice.
They used a mysterious
power called the Force to
defend those in peril.
But nearly all of the Jedi
were destroyed by the Empire.
Who will defend the
galaxy now?

Rebellion!

People are rising up all
across the galaxy to rebel
against the Empire.
They want to be free.

They want to bring back peace
and happiness to the galaxy.
These rebels are determined
to fight for a better future, no
matter how long it takes!

The Rebels of Lothal

On the planet Lothal, a small group of feisty rebels is fighting to make life hard for the Empire.

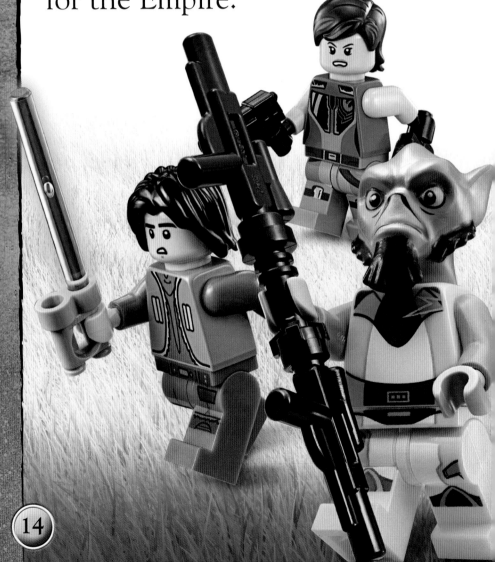

They enjoy blowing up starships
and fooling stormtroopers.
These rebels know it will be
a long fight, but one day they
hope the galaxy will be free.

THE FIRST REBELS

The Empire has done everything it can to destroy the rebels of Lothal. But the six rebels always manage to escape the Imperial officers!

KANAN

Jedi and rebel leader

Good at: Planning missions and using the Force

Weapons: Lightsaber and a blaster

Rebel tactic: Using his lightsaber lightning-fast

EZRA

Jedi-in-training

Good at: Crawling through tiny spaces

Weapon: Lightsaber that is also a blaster

Rebel tactic: Being sneaky and running really, really fast

SABINE

Explosives expert and artist

Good at: Making explosives

Weapons: Twin blasters and explosives

Rebel tactic: Blowing up the Empire's property

Ace pilot and Captain of the *Ghost*

Good at: Keeping the team together

Weapon: Blaster

Rebel tactic: Flying the rebels out of tricky situations

HERA

ZEB

Highly trained Lasat warrior

Good at: Hand-to-hand combat

Weapon: Bo-rifle

Rebel tactic: Being stronger than everyone else

Astromech droid

Good at: Fixing the *Ghost* and keeping it running

Weapon: Booster rocket

Rebel tactic: Distracting the Empire's soldiers and zapping droids

CHOPPER

A New Hope!

The rebels have fought
the Empire for years.
They have caused lots of
trouble for the Empire, but have
still not managed to destroy it.
Now a Rebel Alliance has
been formed. It has a special
member named Luke Skywalker.
This brave young man may
finally be able to defeat
the Emperor.

THE REBEL ALLIANCE

LUKE SKYWALKER
Farm boy and Jedi

Expert at flying the
X-wing starfighter

Can't wait to use the Force
to help his friends

EMPIRE BEWARE
Luke is great
at blowing up
Imperial
starfighters.

EMPIRE BEWARE
Leia is good
at stealing
secret plans.

LEIA ORGANA
Senior rebel leader and princess

Knows exactly how to beat
up stormtroopers

Thinks Han is handsome, but
very rude and not at all funny

The Empire had better be scared of the Rebel Alliance. So what if its members include a farm boy, a smuggler, a princess, and a Wookiee? Together, they are unbeatable!

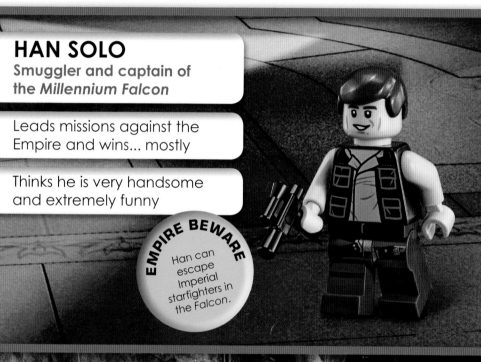

HAN SOLO
Smuggler and captain of the *Millennium Falcon*

Leads missions against the Empire and wins... mostly

Thinks he is very handsome and extremely funny

EMPIRE BEWARE
Han can escape Imperial starfighters in the Falcon.

EMPIRE BEWARE
Stormtroopers should avoid being around when Chewie loses his temper.

CHEWBACCA
Wookiee warrior and copilot of the *Millennium Falcon*

Will do anything for friends, even fight stormtroopers

Likes Jedi and fixing broken droids

A Secret Weapon

The rebels have really been
making Darth Vader sweat.
Now Vader is ready to fight
back with the Death Star.
It is a weapon so deadly that
it can destroy entire planets!
What Darth Vader
doesn't know yet is
that a smart rebel
named Princess
Leia has stolen
the plans for
how the Death
Star works.

REBEL STARFIGHTERS

These mighty starfighters are ready for battle, whether on the icy-cold planet of Hoth, or over the jungles of Yavin 4. The rebels are ready to fly!

X-wing

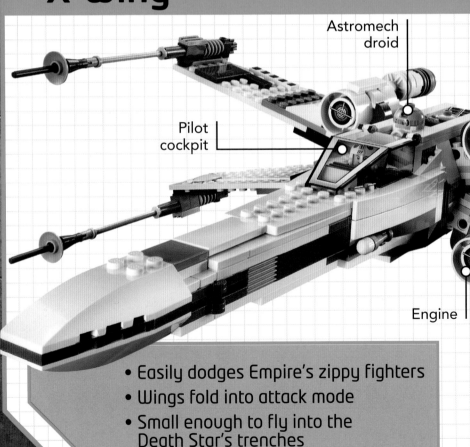

Astromech droid

Pilot cockpit

Engine

- Easily dodges Empire's zippy fighters
- Wings fold into attack mode
- Small enough to fly into the Death Star's trenches

A-wing

The high-speed A-wing is perfect for quick attacks.

One of four wings

Laser gun

B-wing

The B-wing is loaded with missiles and weapons.

Destroying the Death Star

The rebels use the Death Star's plans to find its weak spot. This is the X-wing pilots' only chance. Their best pilot, Luke Skywalker, flies his X-wing at the Death Star. He blows it to pieces in a single shot!

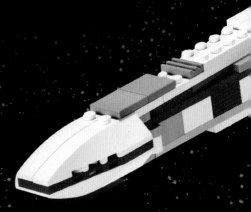

Luke's Diary

Day 48
After we blew up
the Death Star,
Darth Vader was so angry that we decided
the best thing would be to hide. So we
built this base on Hoth. Boy, it is cold!

I had to do some quick Jedi tricks to escape the hungry wampa!

Day 51
Yesterday, I stuck my tongue out and it turned
into an icicle! A few days before that, I was out
on my tauntaun and got kidnapped by this scary
wampa creature. I'm not crazy about Hoth.

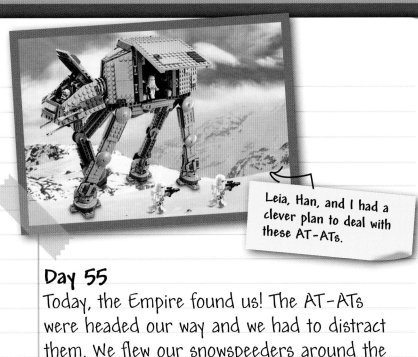

Leia, Han, and I had a clever plan to deal with these AT-ATs.

Day 55

Today, the Empire found us! The AT-ATs were headed our way and we had to distract them. We flew our snowspeeders around the AT-ATs, wrapping cables around their legs. Some of them toppled over. We escaped while they were untangling themselves. Take that, Darth Vader!

Rescue Mission

The Empire has
captured Han Solo.
Darth Vader has frozen
him in carbonite.
Han is not very happy.
He is alive, but trapped!
The rebels don't abandon
their friends, so Lando and
Leia disguise themselves
and stage a daring rescue.
Han knew he could count
on his friends!

MOON OF ENDOR

A REPORT FOR
The Evil Empire

GOAL: To find out if the forest moon of Endor is a good place to put the shield generator for the Empire's new Death Star.

ORDERED BY:
Emperor Palpatine

LOCATION: Far away in an unexplored part of the galaxy. Close to the Death Star.

WEATHER: Mild. Not too hot or cold. A very cool breeze, too.

POPULATION: Mainly short, furry creatures called Ewoks. Do not cuddle them. They bite.

LAND: Thick green forest made up of very, very tall trees. Be careful while riding speeder bikes.

RESULT:
Endor is the perfect place! The tall trees will keep the shield generator hidden. It will be safe from the rebels, who will never be able to find it. The Ewoks use spears. They are no match for the Empire's blasters.

APPROVED

Ewok Attack!

The rebels are under attack from stormtroopers on Endor. The Ewoks, who live there, decide to help the rebels.

They launch sticks and stones
to distract the stormtroopers.
With the stormtroopers off their
guard, the rebels can attack.
They destroy the shield generator
that protects the new Death Star.

Luke has found out that Darth Vader is his father! Now the Emperor is making them fight. Could this finally be...

THE END OF THE
EMPIRE!

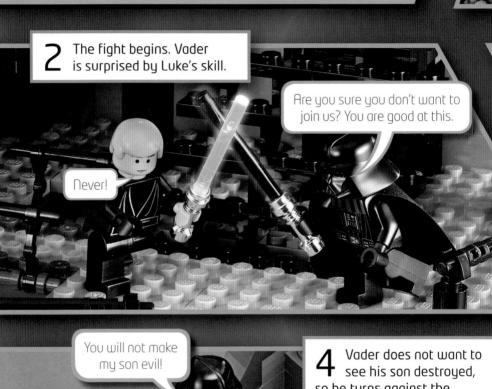

2 The fight begins. Vader is surprised by Luke's skill.

Are you sure you don't want to join us? You are good at this.

Never!

You will not make my son evil!

4 Vader does not want to see his son destroyed, so he turns against the Emperor to protect Luke.

Bye-bye.

Aaaaaa!

Freedom Returns

The Empire has been defeated, thanks to each and every rebel's heroic efforts. The rebels can now celebrate, as fireworks light up the sky.

Our heroes will face more
challenges in the future.
The dark side is
never far away.
But for now, all is well
and the galaxy is free.

ARt YOU A REBtL!

Emperor Palpatine was very powerful, but he only cared about himself. The rebels fought for freedom and to protect others. What would you do? Which side are you on?

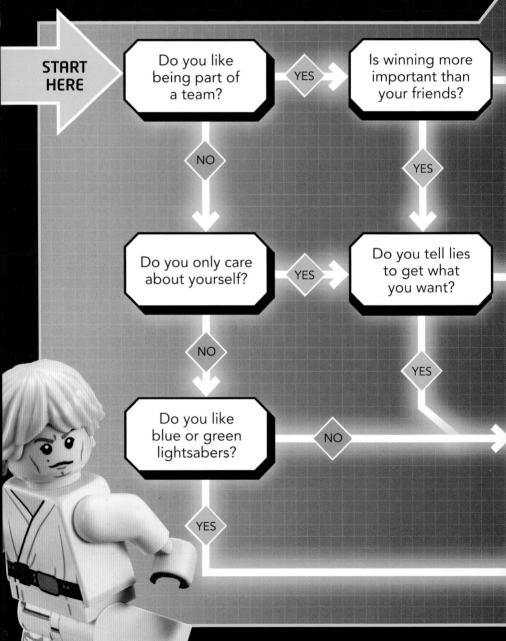

START HERE

Do you like being part of a team?

YES → Is winning more important than your friends?

NO ↓

YES ↓

Do you only care about yourself?

YES → Do you tell lies to get what you want?

NO ↓

YES ↓

Do you like blue or green lightsabers?

NO →

YES ↓

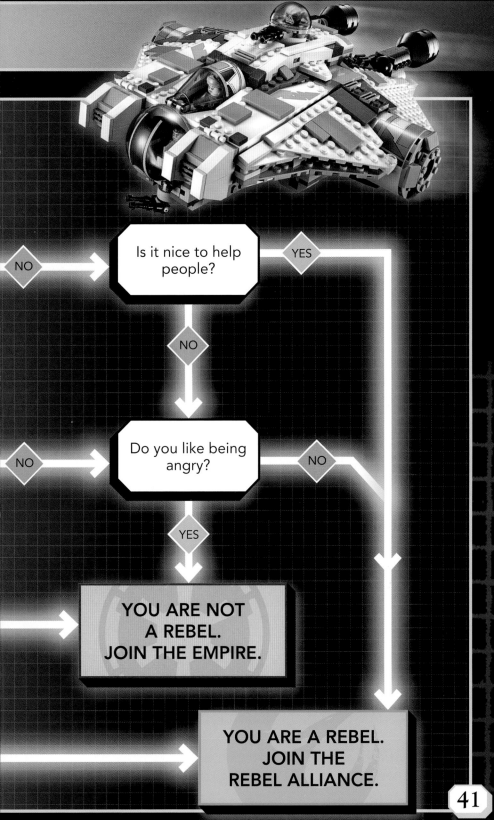

NO →

Is it nice to help people?

YES

NO

Do you like being angry?

NO

NO

YES

YOU ARE NOT A REBEL. JOIN THE EMPIRE.

YOU ARE A REBEL. JOIN THE REBEL ALLIANCE.

Quiz

1. Who are the two dark lords who have taken over the galaxy?

2. On Empire Day, how long had the Empire ruled the galaxy?

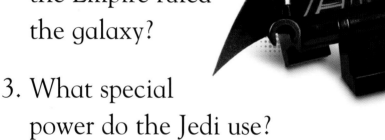

3. What special power do the Jedi use?

4. Which rebel of Lothal uses a bo-rifle as his weapon?

5. Who is the Rebel Alliance's special member?

6. Who steals the plans to the Death Star?

7. Which team of pilots help Luke destroy the first Death Star?

8. Which furry creature kidnaps Luke on Hoth?

9. Where do the Ewoks live?

10. Who is Luke Skywalker's father?

Answers
on page 45

Glossary

Alliance
A union between people who share a common interest

Apprentice
A person who is learning a skill

Citizen
A person who lives in a city or town

Droid
A type of robot

Heroic
Brave

Imperial
Relating to the Empire

Insignificant
Not important

Peril
Serious danger

Radiant
Looking bright and happy

Smuggler
Someone who transports things secretly so they can make money from selling them

Starship
A vehicle used for travel between stars

Index

Answers to the quiz on pages 42 and 43:
1. Emperor Palpatine and Darth Vader
2. 14 years 3. The Force 4. Zeb 5. Luke Skywalker
6. Princess Leia 7. X-wing pilots 8. Wampa creature
9. Moon of Endor 10. Darth Vader

Guide for Parents

This book is part of an exciting four-level reading series for children, developing the habit of reading widely for both pleasure and information. These chapter books have a compelling main narrative to suit your child's reading ability. Each book is designed to develop your child's reading skills, fluency, grammar awareness, and comprehension in order to build confidence and engagement when reading.

Ready for a *Level 2* book

YOUR CHILD SHOULD

- be familiar with using beginning letter sounds and context clues to figure out unfamiliar words.
- be aware of the need for a slight pause at commas and a longer one at periods.
- alter his/her expression for questions and exclamations.

A VALUABLE AND SHARED READING EXPERIENCE

For many children, reading requires much effort, but adult participation can make this both fun and easier. So here are a few tips on how to use this book with your child.

TIP 1 Check out the contents together before your child begins:

- read the text about the book on the back cover.
- flip through the book and stop to chat about the contents page together to heighten your child's interest and expectation.
- make use of unfamiliar or difficult words on the page in a brief discussion.
- chat about the nonfiction reading features used in the book, such as headings, captions, lists, or charts.

TIP 2 Support your child as he/she reads the story pages:

- give the book to your child to read and turn the pages.

- where necessary, encourage your child to break a word into syllables, sound out each one, and then flow the syllables together. Ask him/her to reread the sentence to check the meaning.

- when there's a question mark or an exclamation mark, encourage your child to vary his/her voice as he/she reads the sentence. Demonstrate how to do this if it is helpful.

TIP 3 Chat at the end of each page:

- ask questions about the text and the meaning of the words used. These help to develop comprehension skills and awareness of the language used.

A FEW ADDITIONAL TIPS

- Always encourage your child to try reading difficult words by themselves. Praise any self-corrections, for example, "I like the way you sounded out that word and then changed the way you said it, to make sense."

- Try to read together everyday. Reading little and often is best. These books are divided into manageable chapters for one reading session. However, after 10 minutes, only keep going if your child wants to read on.

- Read other books of different types to your child just for enjoyment and information.

Series consultant, **Dr. Linda Gambrell**, Distinguished Professor of Education at Clemson University, has served as President of the National Reading Conference, the College Reading Association, and the International Reading Association.